FANTASTIC SCIENCE JOURNEYS

A TRIP TO THE
CENTER OF THE
EARTH

BY JANEY LEVY

Gareth Stevens
PUBLISHING

Please visit our website, www.garethstevens.com. For a free color catalog of all our high-quality books, call toll free 1-800-542-2595 or fax 1-877-542-2596.

Library of Congress Cataloging-in-Publication Data

Levy, Janey, author.
A trip to the center of the Earth / Janey Levy.
    pages cm. — (Fantastic science journeys)
Includes bibliographical references and index.
ISBN 978-1-4824-2010-4 (pbk.)
ISBN 978-1-4824-2009-8 (6 pack)
ISBN 978-1-4824-2011-1 (library binding)
1. Earth (Planet)—Internal structure—Juvenile literature. 2. Planets—Geology—Juvenile literature. 3. Geology—Juvenile literature. I. Title.

QE509.L47 2015
551.1'1—dc23

2014029735

Published in 2015 by
Gareth Stevens Publishing
111 East 14th Street, Suite 349
New York, NY 10003

Copyright © 2015 Gareth Stevens Publishing

Designer: Sarah Liddell
Editor: Ryan Nagelhout

Photo credits: Cover, pp. 1, 7 (main), 8, 27 Johan Swanepoel/Shutterstock.com; p. 5 MarcelClemens/Shutterstock.com; p. 7 (cherries) Valentyn Volkov/Shutterstock.com; p. 11 ThomasPusch/Wikimedia Commons; p. 13 Josemaria Toscano/Shutterstock.com; p. 15 (main) Encyclopaedia Britannica/UIG/Getty Images; p. 15 (*Deepsea Challenger*) Imeh Akpanudosen/Getty Images Entertainment/Getty Images; p. 17 Andrei Kukla/Shutterstock.com; pp. 19 (main), 21 (main), 23 (main), 25 leonello calvetti/Shutterstock.com; p. 19 (volcano) Pablo Hidalgo/Shutterstock.com; p. 21 (*Journey to the Center of the Earth*) John Bryson/The LIFE Images Collection/Getty Images; p. 23 (iron) Alena Brozova/Shutterstock.com; p. 29 Blend Images/Shutterstock.com.

Printed in the United States of America

CPSIA compliance information: Batch #CW15GS: For further information contact Gareth Stevens, New York, New York at 1-800-542-2595.

CONTENTS

A Fantastic Field Trip 4

Know Before You Go 6

Cracking the Crust 10

Moving Through the Mantle 16

Boring into the Core 22

Amazing Earth 28

Glossary 30

For More Information 31

Index 32

Words in the glossary appear in **bold** type the first time they are used in the text.

A FANTASTIC FIELD TRIP

What's the best field trip you've ever taken?

Maybe you visited a zoo or went to see works of art.

What if you could board a special ship and explore

Earth's **interior** by traveling all the way down to the

center? That would be an awesome adventure! And this

book will take you on just such a journey.

First, however, you need to know something about

the **structure** of Earth's interior. That way, you know

what to expect and can prepare properly.

THAT'S FANTASTIC!

Plan for a long trip. It's about 3,960 miles (6,370 km) from Earth's surface to the center. That's about the same as the **distance** from New York City to Berlin, Germany.

Earth looks blue from space
because water covers more than 70 percent of
the surface. Your trip will start on land to avoid the
problem of diving to the ocean floor.

5

KNOW BEFORE YOU GO

Earth's interior has **layers**. Scientists often talk about the layers in terms of their composition, or what matter they're made of. Earth has three compositional layers, somewhat like a cherry: a thin outer layer, a thick middle layer, and a solid center.

Scientists also separate Earth's interior into layers based on **physical** properties, or how the matter acts. Earth has five physical layers. Look on pages 8 and 9 to learn the names and features of both types of layers.

THAT'S FANTASTIC!

As you travel down through Earth's layers, the temperature becomes hotter and the **pressure** becomes greater. But don't worry—your special ship will keep you safe on this field trip.

Since no one has actually made a trip to the center of Earth, how do we know about the layers? Scientists have learned about them by measuring how waves created by **earthquakes** travel through Earth.

THE EARTH'S LAYERS

COMPOSITIONAL LAYERS

PHYSICAL LAYERS

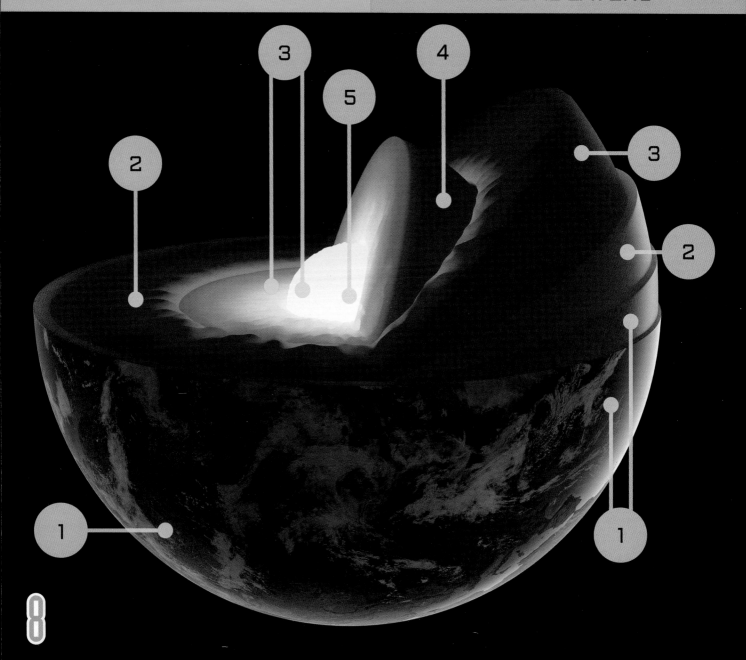

COMPOSITIONAL LAYERS

1. thin crust; rocks made mostly of **silica**

2. thick mantle; silica, iron, magnesium

3. thick core; iron, nickel, oxygen, sulfur

PHYSICAL LAYERS

1. lithosphere; made up of crust and upper part of mantle; solid, stiff

2. asthenosphere; a thin layer of upper mantle; soft solid that can flow

3. mesosphere; most of the mantle; solid that flows, but more slowly than asthenosphere

4. outer core; most of the core; liquid

5. inner core; the center of Earth; solid

9

CRACKING THE CRUST

Earth actually has two types of crust. The continental crust that supports the major landmasses is 18.6 to 43.5 miles (30 to 70 km) thick. It's mostly made of silica in the form of extremely hard rock called granite.

The crust under the oceans is thinner—only 3.1 to 6.2 miles (5 to 10 km) thick. But it's **denser** than the continental crust and has less silica and more iron and magnesium. It's made mostly of hard rock called basalt.

THAT'S FANTASTIC!

How hard is granite? It's hard enough to scratch glass. Ancient Egyptians used it to cut statues that have survived for 4,000 years.

The crust is up to 28 miles (45 km) thick in the Rocky Mountains, 37 miles (60 km) thick in the Andes Mountains, and 43 miles (70 km) thick in the Himalayas!

continental crust

ocean

oceanic crust

11

Your journey will start by tunneling through the crust. The oceanic crust may be thinner, but it's denser and harder to reach. So you'll board your ship on the coast of North America, where the crust is about 18.6 miles (30 km) thick.

That may sound like a lot of rock to travel through, but this is the easy part of the trip. The crust is the thinnest layer of Earth and makes up less than 1 percent of Earth's mass.

THAT'S FANTASTIC!

The crust is broken into pieces called tectonic [tehk-TAH-nihk] plates. These plates move continuously, but so slowly you don't notice it. They move more slowly than your fingernails grow!

The Grand Canyon in Arizona is about a mile (1.6 km) deep. You'll travel more than 18 times that far as you pass through the crust!

13

Remember, temperature and pressure increase as you go deeper. Imagine the surface temperature is 70°F (21°C) when your journey starts. The surface pressure, called air pressure, is 14.7 pounds per square inch (1 kg per sq cm).

At the bottom of the crust, the temperature will be about 800°F (427°C)—hot enough to melt lead! The rock above you will create a pressure of about 183,750 pounds per square inch (12,500 kg per sq cm)—enough to squash the strongest **submarine**. Yikes!

THAT'S FANTASTIC!

At the bottom of the crust, you'll come to a border that separates the crust from the mantle. It's called the Mohorovicic [maw-hawr-aw-VEE-cheech] **discontinuity**, or Moho for short.

Deepsea Challenger

A submarine named *Deepsea Challenger* was built to go deeper in the ocean and to withstand greater pressure than any other submarine. Even it isn't as strong as your ship needs to be.

continental crust

ocean

oceanic crust

Mohorovicic discontinuity

mantle

MOVING THROUGH THE MANTLE

When your ship first enters the mantle, it feels much like traveling through the crust did. That's because, as you read earlier, the uppermost part of the mantle is stiff rock that can break, just like the crust. Together, the two form what's called the lithosphere.

When you look out your ship's window, you notice this part of the mantle is darker and denser than the crust. That's because it's made of a rock called peridotite and includes more iron and magnesium.

THAT'S FANTASTIC!

The word "lithosphere" comes from Greek words that mean "sphere (ball) of rock." It was first used in 1887.

By the time you reach the bottom of the lithosphere, you'll be about 93 miles (150 km) below the surface. That's 86 miles (138 km) deeper than the deepest part of the ocean!

crust

lithosphere

outer mantle

17

As you leave the lithosphere, you enter the part of the mantle called the asthenosphere. The composition remains the same, but you notice a big change in physical properties. The rock is soft and plastic-like. It can actually flow, much like tar you might see on the road.

Great heat makes the asthenosphere flow. It's about 1,900°F (1,040°C)—hot enough to melt silver! The pressure is also huge—about 735,000 pounds per square inch (50,000 kg per sq cm).

THAT'S FANTASTIC!

The word "asthenosphere" comes from Greek words that mean "weak sphere." It was first used in 1914.

The lava, or melted rock, that comes out of **volcanoes** comes from the asthenosphere.

volcano

asthenosphere

19

From the asthenosphere, your ship enters the lower mantle, or mesosphere. It's a good thing your ship can keep you safe, because it's about 3,630°F (2,000°C). That's hot enough to melt iron! But even though it's so hot, the mesosphere is stiffer than the asthenosphere because the pressure is so great. It's 1.4 million times the pressure on Earth's surface!

At the bottom of the mantle, you come to a border separating it from the core. It's called the Gutenberg discontinuity.

THAT'S FANTASTIC!

Altogether, the parts of the mantle make up about 66 percent of Earth's mass. That's more than 66 times what the crust makes up!

French writer Jules Verne imagined a trip to Earth's center in his famous 1864 book *A Journey to the Center of the Earth*, which has been made into movies and TV shows. Verne imagined giant caves, rivers, and creatures from the age of dinosaurs inside Earth.

Journey to the Center of the Earth

mesosphere

BORING INTO THE CORE

After passing through the Gutenberg discontinuity, your ship enters the outer core. Immediately, you notice a huge difference. The outer core is liquid! How is that possible? It's because of the extreme heat. The temperature is about 9,000°F (5,000°C)—more than 10 times as hot as the surface of Mercury and Venus, the two hottest planets in the **solar system**!

The composition of the outer core also differs from that of the mantle. It's made mostly of iron and nickel, with some sulfur and oxygen.

THAT'S FANTASTIC!

The motion of the liquid iron outer core is what creates Earth's magnetic field. The magnetic field keeps Earth safe from harmful rays that come from space.

The outer core outside your ship might look something like the hot, liquid iron in a factory.

outer core

The outer core is about 1,400 miles (2,250 km) thick. The motion of the hot, liquid iron carries your ship along sideways, slowing your travel downward.

Finally, you reach the bottom of the outer core. Here, the temperature is about 10,800°F (6,000°C). That's as hot as the surface of the sun! And the pressure is almost unimaginable. It's about 3.3 million times what it is on Earth's surface! You would never survive without your special ship.

THAT'S FANTASTIC!

The core may be deep inside Earth, but it was the first part of Earth's interior scientists discovered. R. D. Oldham found it in 1906 by studying earthquake records.

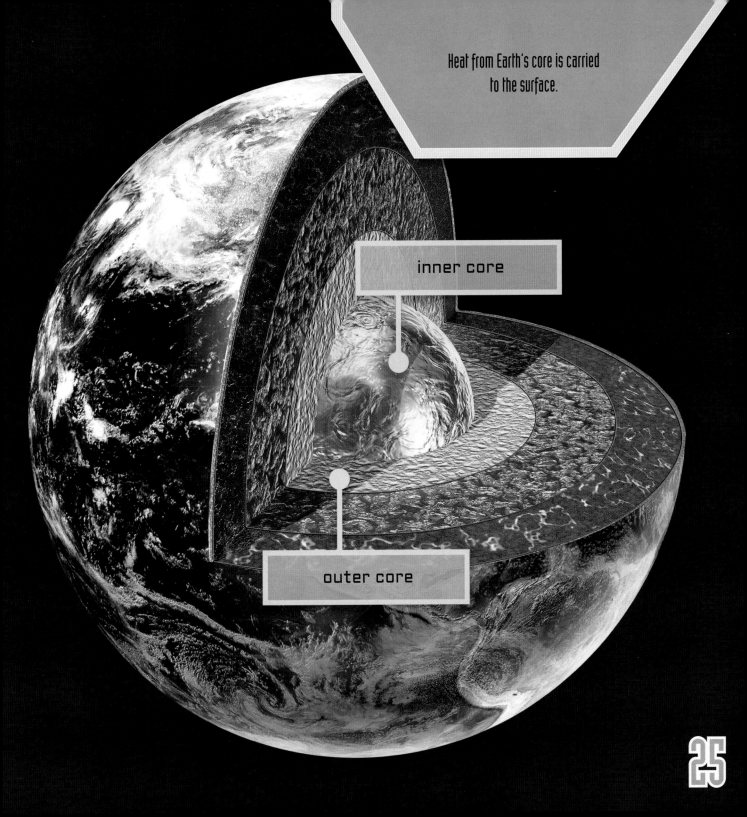

Heat from Earth's core is carried to the surface.

inner core

outer core

25

You're near the end of your journey to Earth's center. Your ship enters the inner core. Its composition matches the outer core, but everything else has changed.

The inner core is the hottest part of Earth's interior, with temperatures up to 12,600°F (7,000°C). In spite of this, it's solid, not liquid like the outer core. Why? It's because of the extreme pressure. The pressure is 3.5 million times that on Earth's surface—enough to keep the white-hot iron from melting!

THAT'S FANTASTIC!

The outer and inner cores rotate, or spin, in opposite directions. The outer core rotates toward the west, the inner core toward the east.

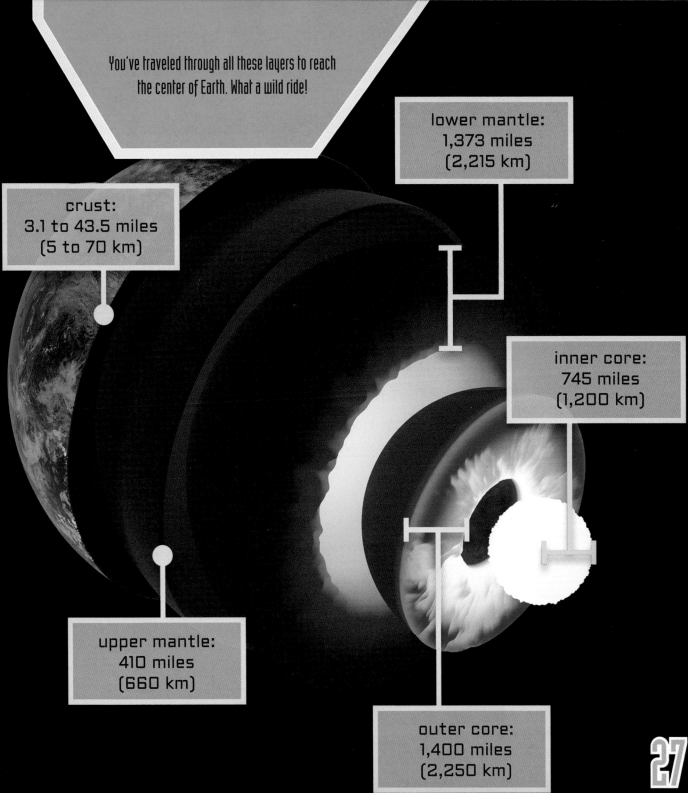

You've traveled through all these layers to reach the center of Earth. What a wild ride!

lower mantle:
1,373 miles
(2,215 km)

crust:
3.1 to 43.5 miles
(5 to 70 km)

inner core:
745 miles
(1,200 km)

upper mantle:
410 miles
(660 km)

outer core:
1,400 miles
(2,250 km)

27

AMAZING EARTH

After you reach the inner core, your ship turns around, takes you back up through Earth's layers, and returns you to your classroom. What an awesome adventure it's been!

You've seen Earth as no one has ever seen it before. It's nothing like the world Jules Verne imagined so long ago, but it's just as wonderful. It has solid, stiff rock; soft, plastic rock; rock so hot it's liquid; and superhot rock under such great pressure it can't melt. It's truly amazing!

THAT'S FANTASTIC!

Some scientists think the inner core may be a single giant crystal of iron.

The next time you're out enjoying a beautiful summer day, think of the amazing, mysterious world beneath you.

GLOSSARY

dense: packed very closely together

discontinuity: a change or break in something

distance: the amount of separation between two points

earthquake: a shaking of the ground caused by the movement of Earth's crust

interior: inside

layer: one thickness of something lying over or under another

physical: having to do with natural science

pressure: a force that pushes on something else

silica: the hard matter that makes up quartz and sand

solar system: the sun and all the space objects that orbit it, including the planets and their moons

structure: the way parts of an object are arranged

submarine: a ship built to operate underwater

volcano: an opening in a planet's surface through which hot, liquid rock sometimes flows

FOR MORE INFORMATION

BOOKS

Green, Jen. *3-D Explorer: Planet Earth—A Journey from the Core to the Skies.* San Diego, CA: Silver Dolphin Books, 2009.

Munsey, Lizzie. *My Tourist Guide to the Center of the Earth.* London, United Kingdom: DK, 2013.

Nemeth, Jason D. *Earth's Layers.* New York, NY: PowerKids Press, 2012.

WEBSITES

About the Earth
geography4kids.com/files/earth_intro.html
This website for kids investigates the layers of Earth and how they work.

How the Earth Works
science.howstuffworks.com/environmental/earth/ geophysics/earth.htm
Learn all about Earth, find helpful diagrams, and see some amazing photos.

INDEX

asthenosphere 9, 18, 19, 20

compositional layers 6, 9

core 9, 20, 24, 25

crust 9, 10, 11, 12, 13, 14, 16

earthquakes 7, 24

Gutenberg discontinuity 20, 22

inner core 9, 26, 28

iron 9, 10, 16, 22, 23, 24, 26, 28

Journey to the Center of the Earth, A 21

liquid 9, 22, 23, 24, 26, 28

lithosphere 9, 16, 17, 18

magnesium 9, 10, 16

magnetic field 22

mantle 9, 14, 16, 18, 20, 22

mesosphere 9, 20

Mohorovicic discontinuity 14

nickel 9, 22

Oldham, R. D. 24

outer core 9, 22, 23, 24, 26

oxygen 9, 22

physical layers 6, 9

pressure 6, 14, 15, 18, 20, 24, 26, 28

silica 9, 10

solid 9, 26, 28

sulfur 9, 22

temperature 6, 14, 18, 20, 22, 24, 26

Verne, Jules 21, 28